7 STEPS

FROM

PROBLEM TO PEACE

A Simple Guide On How To Partner With God In Your Decision Making Process.

THERESA PANG

First Paperback edition June, 2023

Manufactured in the United States of America

Published by Victory Vision
Publishing and Consulting, LLC
www.victoryvision.org

ISBN: 979-8-9883865-0-6 (paperback)
ISBN: 979-8-9883865-1-3 (eBook)

All Bible references cited from the *Holy Bible*.
New International Version,
Zondervan Publishing House, 2011.

TABLE OF CONTENTS

7 STEPS FROM PROBLEM TO PEACE

Are you afraid of making the wrong decisions? Do you lack peace about the decisions you *do* make? How would you like to learn how to partner with the Prince of Peace in your decision making?

You're reading this book because you want to find peace in your problem. Are you ready to jump right into this? We are going to walk through these 7 Steps together.

No one ever said that life would be easy. Making decisions are part of our everyday life. In fact, we will all have trials and tribulations in our life. The key to success is how we move from problem to peace in all areas of our lives and how resilient we are in trying again after we have felt so defeated. What if we reframed our thinking and focused not on the problem but focused on how we are now given an opportunity to find solutions with the Prince of Peace, Jesus Christ? Focus on a mind-set that centers on the solution, not the problem.

> Jesus says, *"I have told you these things, so that in me you may have peace. In this world you will have trouble. But take heart! I have overcome the world"* (John 16:33).

In my career, I have had the opportunity to work with highly esteemed executives and leaders in the California Bay Area while working for various technology companies and have also led a Christian ministry school. From making decisions in boardrooms to planning church services and ministry classes, some decisions often need to be made quickly. The most important constant for me as a believer, which I found myself continuously asking myself, was, "God, am I honoring you? What do you think about this, God? Am I making the right decision? Is this what you want?"

Here are 7 easy steps I have used that have helped me be quick on my feet in my decision-making process, from the corporate world to the ministry sphere. These steps leave me with peace; afterall, Jesus is the Prince of Peace!

Peace I leave with you; my peace I give you. I do not give to you as the world gives. Do not let your hearts be troubled and do not be afraid. — John 14:27

In the Kingdom of God, peace is our inheritance. I believe that when you move in peace, you are literally operating in the midst of God's presence. I hope this strategy will help you find peace in your decision-making process in all areas of your life.

PAUSE

Be still and know that I am God.

— Psalm 46:10

In other words, "Chillax," and just let God be God!

PAUSE: ACTIVATION #1

Let's learn how to pause. First, put your hand on your heart and close your eyes for a minute and focus on your breathing. Take three slow breaths as you turn your spirit and soul inwards and allow this pause to shed all the distractions of the world off your shoulders. Inhale and exhale, counting one to five. Do that three times as you feel your heartbeat pound and your chest rise and fall. Let's try it. Put the book down and stop everything that you are doing now and take a moment to be still.

How did that make you feel? Did intentionally pausing shift anything in your spirit, body, your mind or your heart? Does your mind feel clearer and more relaxed? Do you feel like you can now take on the world?

We're currently living in a pressure cooker and microwave society; we are so conditioned to expect everything to be at our fingertips. Anyone who has operated a pressure cooker can relate to this. A pressure cooker takes a fraction of the time to cook a meal which would normally take hours on a stove top. They call it a pressure cooker for a reason, but before you are able to open the lid and unveil the goodness that's cooking inside of it, you must release the steam. When you're under tremendous pressure, slowing down and repositioning your heart and mind inwards towards God will help you recalibrate and refocus.

From fast food to emails, texts, and social media shorts, being busy has become glorified and a normal part of today's society. We are constantly asking ourselves, how much more can I squeeze into my day?

Have you ever said, "We need more hours in our day?" Did you ever find yourself strategizing on how you can take all your grocery bags from the car to your home in just one trip, no matter how many bags you have? I won't lie, I am certainly guilty of that!

Growing up in America, when I first learned how to cross the streets, I remember learning the commands, STOP, LOOK, and LISTEN. STOP before a crossing, LOOK to the left and LOOK to the right and LISTEN for any oncoming vehicles before you cross. And for fire safety, it was STOP, DROP, and ROLL. If your clothes have caught on fire, first STOP; then DROP to the ground; and ROLL to put the fire out.

Why do you think it is so important to *stop*? When we intentionally pause, it allows us to create momentum for a reset, to refocus and to recalibrate. Let's pause and let God be God.

PAUSE: ACTIVATION #2

What is one particular difficulty or struggle that you are seeking to find a sense of peace or resolution for?

Close your eyes, then take three slow and deep breaths and think of one situation or challenge you are facing and want to find inner peace with. Great! You just completed the first step. Now let's work on finding the solution together with the Lord by walking through these 7 Steps together. Pause, listen and write the situation down.

____

____

____

____

____

____

PRAY

Prayer is powerful. Prayer is our way of communicating with God. We must pray without ceasing.

> *Do not be anxious about anything, but in every situation, by prayer and petition, with thanksgiving, present your requests to God. And the peace of God, which transcends all understanding, will guard your hearts and your minds in Christ Jesus.*
>
> — Philippians 4:6-7

Now that you've taken that time to pause, we are now going to shift our focus to prayer. Invite God into the situation. He is our lifeline. Remember that you are not alone in this world; as believers, the Holy Spirit dwells in you.

Prayer is a direct communication line to God. You have direct access to God, and it is not just a one-way line. When you talk to someone, you'd expect them to respond back. God is the same. In the Bible, He says *"My sheep listen to my voice; I know them, and they follow me"* (John 10:27). If someone is talking to you, how much effort does it take to hear them? You simply hear them; but are you listening to and comprehending what they are saying? Talking to God does not have to be fancy. Talk to God the way you would with a friend.

Prayer will help us shift our stresses, worries, and negative thoughts. It helps us to be aware of what seems to be impossible in the natural realm and in our own mindset; and transfer these negative feelings to God, who will then take your burdens from you. Jesus is the God of miracles and solutions—not us.

Come to me, all you who labor and are heavy laden, and I will give you rest.

— Matthew 11:28

PRAY: PRAYER #1

Situate yourself in a comfortable position.
Speak the Lord's Prayer out loud.
This is how Jesus taught us how to pray.

Our Father in heaven,
Hallowed be your name,
Your kingdom come,
Your will be done,
On earth as it is in heaven.
Give us today our daily bread.
And forgive us our debts,
as we also have forgiven our debtors.
And lead us not into temptation,
but deliver us from the evil one.
Amen

(Matthew 6:9-13)

PRAY: PRAYER #2

God, I give thanks and gratitude for
<Insert what you are thankful for>

I give this circumstance to you.
<Insert situation you are seeking a solution to>

I need you, show me your ways, give me your
strategies and direction.
I want to see from your perspective.
Speak, Lord, for I, your servant, am listening.
I declare breakthrough in this area.
I declare that "The joy of the Lord is my strength"
(Neh. 8:10).
I "walk by faith and not by sight" (2 Cor. 5:7);
for I know that greater is He who is in me than he who
is in the world (1 John 4:4).
I will not fear, because my God is with me.
(Isaiah 41:10) I can do all things through Christ
who strengthens me (Phil 4:13).
Amen.

PRAY: ACTIVATION

Pause and simply wait, listen and write any insights down:

How willing and ready are you to surrender your current challenges to God and why?

____

____

____

____

Where do you still doubt that God will show up in this situation?

____

____

____

____

____

What is the most desirable outcome you are hoping for in this circumstance?

____

____

____

____

____

____

PRAISE

As you continue in prayer, we are going to slowly shift our prayer to praise and worship.

Praise is an offering and sacrifice to God and worship is an expression of adoration. Shift the focus of your prayer to praise, worship, gratitude and thankfulness. We need to rejoice, always! We don't just go to God when we are in need. Can you praise God in your lows and when things are not going the way you want? How do you feel when friends only come to you when they need something from you? God wants a relationship with you, and a relationship is like a garden which needs to be watered, tilled and groomed like any of your relationships here on earth.

Praise the Lord. Give thanks to the Lord, for he is good; his love endures forever.

— Psalms 106:1

Enter his gates with thanksgiving and His courts with praise; give thanks to him and praise his name.

— Psalms 100:4

Merriam-Webster dictionary's definition of *praise* is: *to express a favorable judgment of; or, to glorify, especially by the attribution of perfections.* You will find that praise will help you shift the atmosphere around you, in your heart and in the situation. Begin by declaring the goodness of God with your mouth. Then remind yourself of the miracles and victories you have walked through and start thanking God for the blessings in your life. God has brought you thus far and he will do it again to spring you forward.

The Lord is my strength and my shield; my heart trusts in him, and he helps me. My heart leaps for joy, and with my song I praise him.

— Psalms 28:7

PRAISE: PRAYER

Lord,

I praise you and glorify your name.
Holy, Holy, Holy, Lord God almighty, who was, and
is, and is to come. I worship you, I seek you, I thirst
for you, my lips glorify you, my whole being wants to
be with you; and in your name, I will lift up my hands
and I praise you as long as I live. You are uncondi-
tional love.

I thank you for:
<insert all that you are grateful for>

Amen

PRAISE: ACTIVATION

Pause and simply wait, listen and write any insights down:

How do you feel now after the prayer and reminding yourself of the goodness in your life and past victories?

____

____

____

____

Can you share any new perspectives or understandings that have emerged from focusing on the goodness of your life?

____

____

____

____

PRESENCE

Jesus is alive in you! The manifest presence of God is real and tangible. While the Israelites were in the desert with Moses, God guided them with a cloud by day and fire by night. God also appeared to Moses as a manifested burning bush. In Daniel 3:24-25, when Shadrach, Meshach and Abednego were forced into the fiery burning furnace, King Nebuchadnezzar saw four men. The fourth person was God's manifest presence in the fire.

If you have accepted Jesus in your heart and feel like you have not been able to see or hear God or sense Him physically in your life, let's ask God to show you how real He is! It says in the Bible, draw near to Him and He will draw near to you (James 4:8).

The Word became flesh and made his dwelling among us. We have seen his glory, the glory of the one and only Son, who came from the Father, full of grace and truth.

— John 1:14

When the day of Pentecost came, they were all together in one place. Suddenly a sound like the blowing of a violent wind came from heaven and filled the whole house where they were sitting. They saw what seemed to be tongues of fire that separated and came to rest on each of them. All of them were filled with the Holy Spirit and began to speak in other tongues as the Spirit enabled them.

— Acts 2:1-4

But the Advocate, the Holy Spirit, whom the Father will send in my name, will teach you all things and will remind you of everything I have said to you.

— John 14:26

I keep asking that the God of our Lord Jesus Christ, the glorious Father, may give you the Spirit of wisdom and revelation, so that you may know him better.

— Ephesians 1:17

God's presence comes with rest; and with rest, there is peace. God told Moses, "*My Presence will go with you, and I will give you rest*" (Exodus 33:14). The question now is, "God, am I going where You are going?" Where is God in your life?

Taste and see that the Lord is good; blessed is the one who takes refuge in him.

— Psalm 34:8

Have you tasted his goodness in your life? How do you hear and sense God? We all hear God differently. What is your love language with the Lord? When you are in the Word, reading the Bible, or any book, do the words ever jump out at you, and have you ever had an "aha" moment as deep revelation comes upon you? Have you ever felt goosebumps when something beautiful happens? Do you experience God through nature, sports, movies, music, etc.? Have you ever had a moment when suddenly you got emotional and your eyes filled with tears of overwhelming love or joy? Or a time when you felt an unexplainable peace in a circumstance? Has your gut ever told you that you were at the right place and at the right time or, conversely, have you ever walked into a room and felt like you were not supposed to be there?

Did you ever think of someone randomly and when you reached out to them, they confirmed that it was perfect timing because they really needed someone? Have your hands, feet, or any of your body parts ever felt a sense of tingling, goosebumps, sweat, heat or coldness, or electricity for no reason? Has anyone shared something with you and it was exactly an answer you were seeking for at that particular time? Have you ever felt a weighty presence on your hands, on your shoulders? These may have been God moments.

⁓⁓⁓

Now, let's find out where God is in the situation you are praying into.

PRESENCE: PRAYER

Position Yourself

Sit in a comfortable and relaxed position, and open both hands in a receiving position in front of you as if you are about to receive a gift from someone or lift your arms in the air with your palms open.

Close your eyes, be still, silent, and focus on God or the midpoint between your eyebrows and listen. You are going to take your situation and ask God a few questions. As you ask these questions, simply listen for the first thoughts that come to your mind. Some of you may even get a picture in your head or see a scene played out in its entirety.

PRESENCE: PRAYER

God,

I invite you into my heart and invite you
to this circumstance.
I give this problem to you, Lord.
Thank you, for your presence is with me.
Will you make yourself come alive to me?
Show me where you are in this situation.
I want to taste, see, hear, smell and sense you
everywhere, all the days of my life.
Guide me, Jesus, take the wheel—I want you to
steer my life.

Amen.

PRESENCE: ACTIVATION

Continue with your eyes closed and ask the following questions below. Pause and simply wait, listen and write any insights down:

God, where are you in this situation and what are you doing? What ideas are you getting?

____

____

____

____

Identify any positive aspects or potential benefits of this situation:

____

____

____

____

*If you get nothing, that is okay as well. We can move on to the next step which may give you deeper revelation.

PEOPLE

God's greatest commandment in the Bible can be found in Matthew 22:37-39, which commands us to *love God and love people*. Jesus was the greatest servant of all and his heart obeyed everything God told him to do; and he loved people well.

"There is no greater love than to lay down one's life for one's friends" (John 15:13). God sent his only Son Jesus to die for our sins. The kind of love the Father has for you is undeniably the greatest love we will ever experience. Jesus died on the cross for you. There is no greater love than this.

God commands us to love a friend at all times, to be kind to the poor, to speak up for those who cannot speak for themselves, to defend the oppressed, assist the widows, to bind the broken hearted, heal the sick and release prisoners from captivity. The golden rule is *"do to others what you would have them do to you"* (Luke 6:31).

PEOPLE: PRAYER

God,

Show me everyone involved in this circumstance.

Where are you working presently in those involved in this situation? (Focus on each one or group)

What are you doing in and through these people involved in this situation?

Help me understand the different angles and where these people are coming from. Help me understand their perspective and how they are seeing and understanding this situation.

Amen.

PEOPLE: ACTIVATION

Pause, listen and write any insights down.

Name all the individuals that are part of this situation (directly & indirectly involved):

Let's attempt to see the situation from each of those individuals' perspectives previously listed. Imagine yourself in their place and point of view. What new insights or understanding are you getting from their point of view?

What new perspective have you gotten about your circumstance?

____

____

____

____

____

____

____

____

____

____

PROCESS

The process is the fun part! Are you ready to ask God for his solutions? God says, *"Call to me and I will answer you and tell you great and unsearchable things you do not know"* (Jeremiah 33:3).

All we need to do is ask God. He will provide all the answers to you. I was in the boardroom with a CEO and CFO of a software company once, and in the middle of our conversation, I asked the Lord, "How would you do this?" and suddenly, the entire plan dropped in my head.

In 2020, I was running a ministry school in California and we had planned an in-person conference with ten different speakers. Then the entire country went into the Covid-19 Pandemic shut-down and we had to quickly pivot. We had a leadership meeting and they had asked me to come up with a plan. Online meetings were not as popular back then. I simply freaked out and had no clue what to do; so I put on my baseball cap and went on a walk and started to pray for God's strategy. As I paced back and forth, suddenly, the entire strategy and architecture of the online conference was clear as day to me! I know it did not come from me.

> God says, " . . . *call on me in the day of trouble; I will deliver you, and you will honor me* " (Psalm 50:15).

Call on Him for solutions. He will show you who to partner with and he will give you the strategies. Be silent, listen and wait upon the Lord; for He will give you rest.

Oftentimes, God may even tell you to throw out the process or simply wait because it's not quite the time to take action. He may still be working on the hearts of the people involved—but even in the waiting, He can give rest.

> *Trust in the Lord with all your heart, and do not lean on your own understanding; in all your ways acknowledge him and He will make your paths straight.*
>
> — Proverbs 3:5-6

PROCESS: PRAYER

God,

I can't do this by myself.
I surrender this circumstance to you.
Please take the wheel and guide me.
I give you these burdens and my worries in this
situation.
I give you my control.
Direct me and provide me with your peace and
approach.

Thank you God.
I declare the mind of Christ upon me.
Please give me your creative solutions and strategies.
Thank you, God, for your spirit of wisdom and
revelation in this circumstance.
Amen.

PROCESS: ACTIVATION

What new ideas, resolutions or positive insights did you get? What has shifted in your thinking?

____

____

____

____

____

____

____

____

____

____

____

Based on this new perspective, are you able to formulate a plan and outline a series of practical action steps that you intend to take going forward?

PEACE

You did it! Do you have more peace in your heart with the ideas and solutions you just received in Step 6? Do you have more clarity on the strategies and your next steps in this situation? Thank you, God, for your creative solutions! In the presence of God, there is peace and confidence when you are walking through your circumstances.

Peace I leave with you; my peace I give you. I do not give to you as the world gives. Do not let your hearts be troubled and do not be afraid.

— John 14:27

> *And the peace of God, which transcends all understanding, will guard your hearts and your minds in Christ Jesus.*
>
> — Phil. 4:7

At this time, if you do not have peace in your heart, simply go back to step one: *Pause*.

PRACTICE & REVIEW

The Lord gives strength to his people; the Lord blesses his people with peace.

— Psalm 29:11

As you practice these steps, partnering with God will become a lifestyle to you and you will be able to use them in your everyday life and everything that you do.

I have used these steps not only to ask God to help me with creative solutions in personal areas of my life, but also to survey the room and partner with the Holy Spirit when speaking in a corporate and ministry setting. Being in constant connection with God will give you peace in all you do because you are intentionally connecting with Him.

This is an example of what occurs in my mind and illustrates how my thought process works when I am making quick decisions.

1. Pause – Yes, awkward silence is okay.

2. Pray – *God help me!* What should I do?

3. Praise – *Thank you, Lord, I worship you! Thank you for this person (people) in front of me.*

4. Presence – *Thank you, God, for your presence and being with me in this situation. Guide me, show me what you are doing here at this moment.*

5. People - *God, what is going on in the hearts of these people? Are they hurting? Where are they coming from? (Oftentimes, God may tell me to do nothing and listen, to show them love, and throw out what is on my agenda. Maybe it's simply not the right time to move on to the Process phase.)*

6. Process - Dependent on Step 5, I either proceed with the predetermined agenda, or ask God for a revised plan which may include waiting because the time is not now.

7. Peace - I ask myself: *Do I have peace now with this situation? If I don't have peace in my heart, I would go back to Step 1 and go through the 7 steps again.*

I believe that when you move in peace, you are partnering and operating in the midst of God's presence. I hope this strategy will help you find peace in your decision-making process in all areas of your life.

Peace I leave with you; my peace I give you. I do not give to you as the world gives. Do not let your hearts be troubled and do not be afraid.

— John 14:27

A Prayer of Gratitude
for the Reader

God,

I thank you for the readers and their hunger to want to hear you and partner with you in their lives. Encounter them with your presence and love and speak to them, for they are listening. Reader, I pray more of God over you and that he will continue to bless you abundantly, so that in all things, at all times, you will have all you need and you will abound in every good work (2 Cor. 9:8). I pray that God will continue to fill you with the Spirit of God, in wisdom, in understanding, in knowledge, and in all craftsmanship (Ex. 35:31)—that wherever God takes you, when you pray, the place where you are all gathered together will be shaken and all will be filled with the Holy Spirit and you would speak the word of God with boldness and for His Glory (Acts 2).

In Jesus' almighty Name,

Amen

BONUS SECTION:

Pilgrimage:
A Journey with Purpose

Although you have reached the end of the book, you're actually beginning a journey!

It's not an easy trip, a stroll in the park, or a casual vacation, it's a journey with purpose: the purpose of growing closer to the Father heart of God. It is a walk with God and God's people, that's why we call it a *pilgrimage*. No matter who you are or what you've done, you're invited!

If you have tried just about everything in life to search for hope and peace in your life and found that nothing has worked, why don't you give Jesus a chance?

Would you like to go on this pilgrimage and get to know Jesus?

PILGRIMAGE: PRAYER

Invitation for Salvation

There is a God in Heaven who sent His only Son to die on the cross for our sins. On the third day, He rose from the dead and dwells in us by the way of the Holy Spirit. If you are reading this book and do not know Jesus Christ, but want to experience Him in your life, and want Him to guide you; if you want to invite Jesus to be the Lord of your life, all you have to do is repeat this prayer:

Salvation Prayer

Lord Jesus, I invite you into my heart and ask you to become the Lord of my life. I am sorry for my sins. Cleanse me, fill me with Your Holy Spirit. Thank you for the sacrifice that you made on the cross for me. I believe you died for my sins and rose from the dead. On this day forward, the past is in the past; and today, I am a new person in Christ. Guide me, take the wheel. I will serve you all the days of my life.

In Jesus' Name, Amen.

PILGRIMAGE: ACTIVATION

Next Steps on the Journey with Jesus as a Christian:

1. Read the Bible

Why? The Bible shares specific stories of the many ways that God has walked with humanity to redeem us, which means God *acted to buy us back* from the clutches of sin. When we read scriptures, we also walk along with the people God chose to tell this story through; we meet them in their pain and difficulty and in their joy of meeting God. As we do so, we learn to meet God for ourselves.

2. Find a Church

And, why find a church? The church is full of imperfect people who are walking in the same direction together. The journey, the walk, or the *pilgrimage* is not something you'll want to go alone. There is power in the experience when we meet God together.

> *I rejoiced with those who said to me, "Let us go to the house of the Lord."*
>
> — Psalm 122:1

> *For where two or three gather in my name, there am I with them.*

> — Matthew 18:20

3. Pray

Pray and connect with God. Learn how to recognize God's voice in your life. The way God speaks to you may be different from the way He speaks to those around us.

4. Grow with Community and Mentors

Growing in a Christian community is a wonderful way to deepen your faith and develop meaningful relationships with others who share the same beliefs. There is something beautiful about growing and thriving in community, service, prayer, and connection together. Attend in-person or watch sermons online, and join a discipleship group at your church where you will find it safe to ask questions, discuss, learn, explore and grow. Additionally, serving in a ministry or volunteering for community service projects can help you connect with others and use your talents to make an impact.

Finally, investing and building one-on-one relationships with other Christians through prayer, fellowship, and accountability can help you stay focused, encouraged and positive in the good times and when you face challenges.

Blessings on your journey as you find peace in all areas of your life and as you lean in to hear God's voice. May there be great breakthroughs as you learn to flow with the Holy Spirit and as he guides and teaches you all the days of your life.

ABOUT THE AUTHOR

Theresa is a faith driven entrepreneur and corporate leader. She is passionate about seeing people walk in their purpose and pursue the Kingdom of God as a lifestyle. She believes that everyone has a unique calling on their life and is committed to serving and helping individuals discover and fulfill their God-given potential to help transform and make a positive impact in the world.

www.ingramcontent.com/pod-product-compliance
Lightning Source LLC
Chambersburg PA
CBHW051335150726
47997CB00004B/1473